Carol Jones was born   ; a
local grammar school at the age of 16 Carol had a variety of jobs and travelled a great deal, sometimes penning poems for her own pleasure. It was not until 2020 and the lockdown that affected the entire world that she began to write poems regularly about the things that were affecting her and how she viewed the world around, turning to nature as she had always found nature reassuring as a child.

For Alan William Jones who will never know how he inspired me to write.

Carol Jones

A STRANGE TIME IN LIFE

AUSTIN MACAULEY PUBLISHERS™

LONDON · CAMBRIDGE · NEW YORK · SHARJAH

A CIP catalogue record for this title is available from the British Library.

ISBN 9781398480285 (Paperback)
ISBN 9781398480292 (Hardback)
ISBN 9781398480308 (ePub e-book)

www.austinmacauley.com

First Published 2023
Austin Macauley Publishers Ltd®
1 Canada Square
Canary Wharf
London
E14 5AA

The Life Rooms, The Everyman Playhouse Liverpool, The Learning Team at the Royal Liverpool Philharmonic Hall and The Canal and River Trust. All these organisations worked together to provide online sessions for wellbeing and these provided the inspiration for much of this book.

Table of Contents

A Poem for a Great Loss

It's late in the day
It's late in a lifetime
There is much to reflect on
There is much more to say
Memories vary
From person to person
Clarity comes with time to look back
See what you didn't see at the time
Dismiss the negative
It no longer matters
Remember the positive
The joy that was shared
The times when helpless with laughter
Tears streaming down faces
Unable to stop
Pictures are snapshots
Reminders to jog
Our memories that
Were lost in the fog
Now looking back

Hearing a song
Seeing an old film
All that was familiar
Can be enjoyed once again.

A Lifetime of Loving Animals

There were the rabbits on the lawn
Seen through the window early morn
The mice that strayed from the field
One in the wardrobe mother squealed
Moles leaving little hills on the lawn
Father unamused he felt such scorn
Dougal, my fox terrier, barking so loudly
Tried to pick up a ball and dropped it soundly
It was a hedgehog defending himself
Dougal shocked, left the scene with stealth
In class aged 10 we set traps with the teacher
So we could study and care for each creature
Voles, shrews and mice to tend for a few days
While we studied their habits and funny ways
Getting older, moving on, was not so much fun
The only creature encountered in grammar school
Was a frog to dissect in the lab which I found cruel
Adulthood arrived and my time with animals grew less
Until I started travelling, and then I felt blessed
On my travels overtime I've encountered many a beast
Living wild and free these were sights on which to feast
Chipmunks, a raccoon, a large elk and a smelly skunk
A pair of playful dassies behaving like they were drunk

Quite a few lizards or geckos and tortoises too
Just ambling along the road with not much to do
Penguins on sun soaked white sand
Nesting chicks kept safe on this land
In the sea a large turtle very close to the shore
So cleverly camouflaged I mistook him for the floor
I have seen many other creatures caged in zoos
Seeing them in the wild is what I prefer to choose.

Where the Canal Begins

The view of the city from under the bridge
In the bright morning light of November
Birds on the water beginning their day
Unaware they are part of such splendour.

Sky and Weather

The sky above is made of gases
Visible both night and day
Red and orange hues greet the night
When the pitch blackness is broken
Only by the glow from the moon
White, grey or black clouds move across the sky
Foretelling changes in the weather
Nature looks to the sky both night and day
The lightness and darkness show the way
When to grow, to blossom, to ripen and rest
To replenish for when growth begins again
The seasons come and go, regular each year
Changing with the light and darkness of the sky
In the north and south they bring new life
Wind blows, the clouds bringing water for all
Because the sky and the light and the weather
Are united in their quest to sustain life on earth.

Under the Sea

Floating above before the descent
To witness what lies below
The water feels warm
There is light, enough to see
Fish swimming around
Such beautiful colours
Loud sounds of the water
Always in motion
Up and down bobbing and weaving
Spun by the water turning to face
A long wiggling creature
Grinning it seemed
Attracted by light shining
Curious to know what shines so bright
Light fades and breath runs out
Almost time for the sun to sink
Below the waves on the horizon
Deep orange and red filling the western sky
Slowly sinking it disappears from sight
Darkness all around now it is night.

Reunion

A well-loved place, happy days of old
Returning now, new sights unfold
It's different now but better too
People returning though they are few

Excited children going on rides
Which one is next? Who decides?
Limited spaces and distanced queues
Anticipation builds like lighting a fuse

A friend I'd not seen for seven years
Looking up from my lunch he appears
The chat was rapid exchanging news
Lots of laughter and opposing views

Another friend joins to share our chat
We find things in common, fancy that!
Reunions with special people and places
Creating memories to put smiles on our faces.

Past Times

Going back to the past, what do we find?
So many memories left far behind
Long days in the sun, playing games, having fun
Memories fading with the passage of time
And far in the future looking back on our lives
Was that how it happened, when brought to mind?
The events that shape us, the twists and the turns
Buried deep in our past yet still causing concern
These fleeting thoughts, how real can they be?
Are they important, insignificant or even reality?
Fixed in time they inform the present and future too
Be grateful for those moments that will not come again
Put away those others that only fill you with shame
Let go of cloudy thoughts, there is no need to explore
A product of our past but the future promises more.

My Friend the Moon

Whatever the time, day or night
I look up to find you there in my sight
On cold mornings, still in darkness
You are there to welcome me
Glowing like a beacon pointing the way
When the sun comes up and lights the sky
You are still there, and I wonder why
Do you ever take a break from your watchful role?
Do you know the joy you bring to your friend below?

Meditation on the Thames

In all my many times in London
Even living there for a while
I never spent time by the river
No time to stop and smile
Our time here is not limitless
Slow down and look around
On walks along the pathways
So much to ponder all around
As each bridge looms above
Below on the water is found
A myriad of sights distracting the mind
Forgetting all life's worries
Take in the vista before your eyes
Memories of years gone by
Eclipsed by a wonderful surprise
To find peace and happiness
Flora and fauna colours like gems
As you meditate on the Thames.

A Walk to the Spiral Steps

I took the train to Litherland and walked on up the hill
Halfway to the swing bridge I was amazed at what I saw
A wall and gable end of a house with captured Beatles so still
On I walked to find the welcome committee of pigeons once
more
A familiar sight now like old friends we greet
When encountering them upon the street
Along the towpath and there he stood, so proud
A Canada goose looking hopefully and calling out so loud
I'm sorry I don't have any food, I must remember next time
Some mallards swimming by, enjoying the sun of a December
sky
Benjamin John the name on a canal boat moored nearby
And on the opposite bank forsythia in bloom and I wonder
why
The seasons seem to merge now and don't obey the rules
Humans have unbalanced nature, as a species we are such
fools
Mallards basking in the sun beneath a blossoming tree
To spend their lives together raising young and being free
A noisy, nosy red beaked bird swims by to see what's going
on
Many other ducks appear all singing their own songs

A signpost for walkers or boats to get their bearings
123 and a 1/4 miles done and only 4 more miles to go,
Looking out across the nearby field a gull and two magpies
Pecking at the grass for food and resting tired wings that took them high.
The little park, trees almost bare in chilly autumnal winds
The hardy magpie is happy enough perched on bright blue fencing
The ironwork below depicting yellow painted fish and reeds bending
Suddenly no sounds to be heard, a peaceful calm descends
Just still water, and trees gently swaying in the breeze
My journey is coming to an end, my walk is almost done
I see ahead the spiral steps where up above the world moves on
But down here by the canal it's quiet with time to appreciate the sun.

Flowers of the Lilac Shrub

The lilac flowers of the lilac shrub
So dainty and numerous seen close-up
And from afar their sweet scent
Borne on the breeze is magnificent
Conjuring memories of far off days
The laughter as children played
Grandma in her lilac pinny
Finds them hiding in the spinney
The sun is sinking in the west
Long days like this were the best
Scents, sounds and colours remain
As memories to be lived again.

Dancing on the Water

In a faraway land on a beach of golden sand
The sun was setting and the night grew dark
The water lapped the shore, as the wind began to blow
Louder and louder came the sound, darker grew the sky
A low rumbling filled the air as raindrops began to fall
A lone figure on the sand ran into the water
As the waves grew larger and the rain began to pour
There was a mighty clap of thunder and the figure dove under
The water as the waves rose higher below the jet black sky
Rising through the swirling waves to a scene as bright as day
The clouds now turned translucent in the shimmering light
As the figure floating on the water taking in the view
Rolling clouds, falling raindrops waves crashing to the shore
How incredible it was witnessing the wondrous show of
nature
Afloat on the waves as the raindrops danced upon the water.

The Abnormal Island

It lies in a violent northern ocean, far from any land.
High seas wreck all vessels destined for the sand.
Inhabited solely by plants, it has a strange tale to tell
Of ancient creatures emerging from below,
To scale the mountains, fell the trees for shelters
Taking plants to feed their insatiable appetites.
The island could not sustain this destruction
Balance had to be restored
And so it came to pass that the plants,
Acting to save their land
Tempted the creatures with new exotic fruits
These fruits were filled with poison
That drove the creatures mad
They staggered from high ground
To reach the beach below
Hurling themselves into the waves
They were swept out to the rocks
Where they foundered, sinking slowly
To meet their inevitable fate
For they should never have emerged
The island is not for them.
The island is abnormal, it takes care of itself
Repels all other creatures who think that they might dwell.

You cannot visit this island
For it can never be found
It appears on no maps but it is there forever
Vanquishing all would be conquerors.

Two Sides to Everything

Who decides which side?
Are there only two to choose?
Are you good or bad?

Believe proven facts
Or ignore and take on faith
What you trust is true

A line that divides
Two halves in opposition
Is one side better?

Do colours divide?
Red and blue make purple too
Unite not divide

Upbeat or downcast
Look at things in other ways
To find peace and hope.

Questions and Answers

Why am I here?
There's nowhere to go
Who can I talk to?
There's no-one to listen
What would I say?
There is nothing to say
When will it end?
There is no end.

Animals

Animals are wondrous, each with a job to do
In harmony with their environment, all their neighbours too
They form a chain, a hierarchy survival of the fittest
From the smallest tick to the mighty blue whale
Each link in the chain is maintaining the balance
Humans are animals who claim to be the smartest
It doesn't take a genius to see they're actually the dumbest
The only species to knowingly destroy its own habitat
No other animal on earth would consider doing that
The shrinking natural world is crying out in pain
Fires, floods, hurricanes, earthquakes are the calls
Please stop and heed these warnings if it's not too late
Year by year life for animals gets harder to maintain
They were content within their roles willing to play the game
Until humans appeared and now nothing is the same
Animals are wondrous each with a job to do
Why not follow their example and adopt their point of view?
That cooperation with all Earth's life forms benefits humans
too.

Are You Not a Star Too?

"I see you looking up at me
Tell me, what do you see?"
"You're a shining light on
A very dark night,
You bring comfort to me."
"Why do you say it's very dark?
Are you speaking of your mood?"
"When I have doubts, it's reassuring
To know that you're still there."
"But what is there for you to doubt?
You travel around your world,
Adored by all your friends
I am but a floating light up in your sky.
You have so much, so why be sad
Are you not a star too?"

Childhood Games

Games played as a child should bring joy
Not always true when you play with a boy
A boy who is older and stronger than you
Who makes the rules, tells you what to do
This isn't fun but complaints go unheard
Hurt and unhappy this is absurd
Why does he do it? Why inflict pain?
No-one to stop him and his cruel games
Always the good guy never the bad
It's acceptable behaviour, he's just a lad
The young girl always on the losing side
Learned from an early age to empathise
Always standing up for the outsiders
Unjustly treated by those who divide us.

Journey of Life

The journey that is life
We know not how long it lasts
We navigate its waters
As naive enthusiasts

Joining fellow travellers
Going the same way
Sometimes for many years
Sometimes for just a day

Finding joy and sorrow
On this wondrous trek
Amid beauty and horror
We are but a speck

Treasure what is beautiful
Keep it in your thoughts
The journey may end suddenly
No warning of any sort.

Signs of Spring

Snowdrops appearing from beneath
A covering of fallen winter leaves.
A pair of mallards on the pond
Looking very much at home.
Leaving to take a walk
To find themselves some food.
Flower buds are opening
To brighten up winter's gloom.
Vivid purple crocuses outshine
Their neighbours with their hue.
Yellow blooming daffodils stand tall
To welcome a season that is new.

The Moon

I look around, it is so dark
The brightest glow obscured
By the lesser orb below
With its multi coloured surface
I see movement and shapes
That change as time passes
The blue areas are larger
Is that my doing alone?
They shrink again
We drift in patterns
Then it all happens again
In a never ending chain
I wonder about the other orbs
Are they thinking the same?

Artistic Perspectives

From the beginning of the universe
On planet earth Homo Sapiens
Have depicted their experiences
In artworks large and small
Colours from plants to paint cave walls
Vast canvasses in galleries
Life from centuries through time
Landscapes of fields with farmers
Toiling in the fields or workers in factories
Smoke billowing from tall chimneys
Around the world they hang on walls
To sit in front of masterpieces
In awe at the artists' craft
Depicting scenes of times gone by
The future too is there to see
In smaller works of art
Vivid colours of landscapes full of animals
Far in the distance the teetering skyscrapers
Falling to earth no longer required
For Homo sapiens have breathed their last
Confined safely to the past.

Birds on the Lake

A clear blue spring sky
Above the rippling water
Graceful swans and geese

Seagulls, pigeons, ducks
Swimming, feeding and preening
As the sun shines down.

Mind and Body

Mind controls the body
But the body disagrees
We should work in harmony
You cannot think away the pain
The mind can help in other ways
To divert you from the ills
By using mind and body
Body and mind will help you heal.

The Myth of Britishness

What is Britishness?
Just an outdated label
The Empire was lost

Scotland, Ireland, Wales
Their Celtic heritage strong
England's hanging on

I love your accent
Travel and that's what you hear
You sound so British

It's nonsense of course
There is no British accent
This land is diverse.

Canal Walking

Late in life, I began to walk the canals to find
My love of nature, photography and walking combined
In urban areas where loud noise abounds
There is plenty of tranquility to be found
Plants along the towpath changing with the seasons
Bare and brown in winter and as frost and ice retreat
Green shoots and buds appear in spring
Birds feathering their nests to welcome their offspring
So many birds on the canal was a pleasant surprise
Geese, swans, cormorants, and many kinds of ducks
Seagulls, pigeons, and magpies also fill the skies
Competing for food they swoop to try their luck
I've wondered what it's like to be a bird
The ability to float, swim, walk or fly seems absurd
Waking with the sun and sleeping with the moon
Communicating through song by singing a happy tune
It's a joy getting to know these birds so well
Looking at their photos I am back under their spell
They make me smile and my worries float away
Walking the canals is a peaceful way to spend your day.

Weeping Willow

Oh weeping willow, tell me what do you see?
Standing there on the towpath so majestically
Through all the seasons you are there
Creating shade in the summer
For walkers to stop and stare
To enjoy the view you frame so well
But what unknown stories could you tell?
Of the life on the canal in all its forms
From birds and other creatures large and small
To the canal boats passing by, do you know where they go?
Or are you content just to observe the constant flow
Of life upon the water sometimes busy, sometimes slow
As daylight fades to dark and moonlight fills the sky
Still, you stand there proudly watching canal life passing by.

Distant Love

Now that love is from a distance
Miles overland and hours ahead
The heart still feels its existence
Love still thrives it is not dead

More distant as time passes
Memories drift in and out
Love comes now in flashes
Yet love lingers without doubt

Love does not end with death
Feelings and thoughts remain
It is there each time we take a breath
In words and deeds it is sustained.

Dreams and Grief

They come to me in my dreams, in my grief
All that I have known and lost, who went before, they come
to me
The first, who should have stayed longer but left
Before I really knew what love from mother to daughter could
be
I'll never know, she comes to me in my grief
I dream of papa who raised me all alone and taught me
strength
And leadership, be brave and get things done.
I followed in his footsteps, never doubting that I should
He was a tough instructor, in life and work and love
As I grew to be a woman, don't give your heart away too soon
It must last a lifetime, he did not want me to suffer grief
As he had done, losing his one true love so young
I was sure my first love was the one that would stand the test
of time
He comes to me now in my dreams, in my grief, he'd gone
away
Papa brought him back to me to have him by my side
For Papa would soon leave himself and could not leave me
alone
He comes to me in my dream now, my first love, in my grief

He could not stay to comfort me, and still in grief I dream
I find solace with another, we are wed and all seems fine
But when we, and all our friends, are in danger for our lives
In that moment, with certain knowledge it was right
Papa died to save us all a little sooner than he might
He comes to me in dreams in my grief to say
Be strong now, for I have fought my last fight.

Where Songs Lead

I left my heart in San Francisco
Saw the lights go down in Massachusetts
Sat on the dock of the bay
Walked the bonnie banks of Loch Lomond
Sailed over the sea to Skye
Travelled back in the USSR
In my Liverpool home
Took a ferry cross the Mersey
Saw the fog on the Tyne
Been walking in Memphis
I didn't cry for Argentina
I have been a wild rover
In Dublin's fair city
Chicago is my kind of town
New York, New York once is not enough
Looked out on the continental divide
Of the rocky mountain high, Colorado
With all the songs that lead somewhere
You'll never walk alone.

Transitions

How quickly time moves in nature
Seasons change from one to the next
As the years fly by
Yet as they pass and we transition
From one age to the next
Still feeling young, our faces do not lie
They show the pain, the joy,
The laughter and sorrow
In every line that appears but goes unnoticed
Until finally, we see that we have become old
We have travelled from birth, towards death
But did not notice the journey
Too busy to wonder at the miracle
That we were ever here at all.

The Waiting Room

The waiting room is a fearful place
Or one of joyful anticipation
Of the journey to come
As you sit there at the station

The other waiting rooms in life
Are more anxious in their purpose
Afraid of what is to come
Keeping feelings below the surface

The largest waiting room of all
The planet we call home
Not knowing when the wait will end
Or where next we will roam.

Sanctuary

Sanctuary can be found
In the most unusual places
Escape the troubles that abound
Travel far, to where you're faceless
The sea of tranquility on the moon
Is where real peace can be found
Floating freely all worries now baseless
No time exists don't leave too soon
No rush to return to solid ground
Sanctuary is a gentle caress
To find comfort and regenerate
Until sanctuary is all around.

Memories

The mind is full of memories
Of good and happy times
Of sad days best forgotten
Fleeting thoughts mere reveries

Tormented by the bad times
Why they are not lost
Like the joyful days forgotten
They should age like fine wines

The mind cannot hold everything,
What is stored is for a reason,
Searching for some meaning,
Will not lead to self-healing.

Each fragment of happiness
Remembered and then gone
Will replace those bad times
Life goes on and they hurt less.

Life Is Learning

Born into a life completely new
Our instincts being our only clue
Helpless when we begin our journey
Senses slow to show the way
Gradually there is some focus
Sight and sounds all around
Imitating what we see
And finding a voice make
Ourselves heard to gain
Attention to be nourished
This is a slow process
Helped or hindered by those close by
The learning has begun
It is a ceaseless process
That takes us through our lives
If we are fortunate we thrive
Those less so fall by the wayside
Learning takes us on the journey
That we choose and we continue
On that journey with nothing to lose
And everything to gain if we
Never stop learning something new.

Lost and Found

Those things that are precious
Keep them somewhere safe
To be treasured forever
Wherever you roam

Those things that are precious
Get lost in the passage of time
Out of reach and replaced
Gathering anew, things are found

Those things that are precious
Collect in the dark recesses of mind
Dreams or reality searching to find
Those things that are precious
Will always be there to be found.

Hope of Liverpool

There is a street called Hope in Liverpool, standing at one end
The Cathedral Church of Christ in Liverpool and at the other end
The Metropolitan Cathedral of Liverpool, half a mile apart they stand
Magnificent works of architecture, a beautiful sight for all to see
They bring joy and comfort to their flocks and when times are hard
They give hope to the City and their faith keeps them strong
Religion, politics and football, frequent sources of rivalry
In times of crisis, when people are divided, Liverpudlians unite
They face a common enemy with spirit for they know what's right
Blue or Red, no matter which colour you wear to show support
The reds and blues stand firm together in this richly creative city,
Celebrated in songs and laughter, its people tell their stories
In many different forms entertaining and uniting people
Far beyond these shores.

Arrival Was a
Long Time Coming

It was an old film in the afternoon where
The most spectacular view appeared
The arrival was first seen

Many years went by missing one chance
Until it came around again by happenstance
The arrival was first seen

In colour now not black and white
Not from below but at a great height
The arrival was first seen

Heart pounding, breathless at the sight below
No more imagination the reality did grow
The arrival was first seen

It did not disappoint, each sight seen from above
Explored close up they are far more than enough
The arrival was first seen

Years later on board ship sailing closer
Breathlessly waiting as shapes appeared
There at last as in the film
The arrival was first seen.

Blue

As blue as the sky or as blue as the sea
Initially is what comes to me
Bluebells and forget-me-nots
A blue carpet, when winter fades away
The vivid blue of the proud peacock's chest
That may be what I love the best
Until I discovered to my delight
Looking upward through the trees
To the bright blue sky beyond
Peacocks climbing branch by branch
To show off their colours from a vast height.

Easter Weekend 1973

Easter Saturday, it should be fine
A great day out now its spring time
But this is England after all
200 miles in the rain to watch football
Me and Al looked like drowned rats
As we entered the bar, got drinks and sat
Lots of friends were already there
In the away fans' bar without a care
Then in comes a mob in black and white
Seemingly intent on starting a fight
We weren't having any such thing
In unison we started to sing
We had walked through the storm
With our heads held high
We were not afraid of the dark
At the end of the storm
We'll be flying high
As the players appear on the park
Let's go, let's go with hope in our hearts
And we'll never go alone
As we stood to watch the game
We took shelter from the rain
Under the largest flag I'd ever seen

The pitch turning slowly to brown from green
All level at one all at the half time whistle
Then a goal down the day became abysmal
Heading to the station for trains to all points south
We sang with heads held high, not down in the mouth
When I arrived back home in Leicester
No-one there to make my tea
Mum and dad away for sun at Easter In
Whitby by the Sea.

Fascination in the Park

So many unexpected sights on a walk around the lake
A female mallard perched halfway up a tree
On closer examination of the scene below
Two male mallards locked in battle to be her beau
It is that time of year again and further round the lake
An island is again preparing to welcome new life
The male swan is gathering long twigs for a new nest
Further still and it appears there are more ducks to see
The very striking black and white tufted ducks
There is one more surprise could it be a fairy's door
So many unexpected sights on a walk around the lake.

Language of Birds

Caw caw! Chirp chirp! Squawk squawk!
Communications of the birds
The variety of vocal sounds
Is not just noise
Each sound has a reason
They warn of danger
Tell of food sources
Fight over territory
Loud and soft
Melodic and tuneful
Each has a purpose
This is their language
Used to great effect
To attract a mate
To keep predators away
This is how they survive each day
So as you walk around and listen
To all these different sounds
They are not singing for pleasure
They are exchanging information

But to hear them in the early morning
Or in the busy months of spring
Brings joy and happiness to many
So please birds, sing, sing, sing.

The Bach Suites

Excitement rising
What lies ahead?
Possibilities
Running through my head

Dreamlike thoughts
So peaceful,
Now and calm

Tapping my feet
I have to dance
Come join the fun!

Emotional Turmoil

An angry storm rages
Filling my head
As loud as thunder
As heavy as lead
Pounding and pounding
With no release
Faster and faster
My heart beats increase
Blood gushing through veins
It seems never to cease
Gain control loose these chains
Escape from these thoughts
That cause all this panic
Be calm now and rest
Breathe slow and steady
Silence the noise
Remove the weight
On my chest
Now, I am calm
Now, I am ready.

What Is the Point?

There is no point in being here
An oft repeated theme
Met with laughter and disdain
But all those who disagreed
Said cheer up and smile
Are not here to see
I can still laugh and find it funny
That they didn't listen
Laughed it off as just a joke
They are not laughing now.

Sounds of Summer

All the colours of the rainbow
Are there for all to see
On the merry-go-round
Children laughing endlessly
Chimes of the ice cream van
The pattering of feet
Music from a radio
Far way down the street
As the sun sinks from sight
A gentle walk on a warm night
Tranquility all around
Gentle lapping of water
Barely making a sound.

Sunrise

A dramatic entry to another day
The sun appearing above the horizon
Painting the black sky in shades of orange
Pale clouds scattered by the glow
Birds happily heralding its arrival
Plants turning skyward and buds opening
As hope and excitement fill the air
Here the earth comes alive
On the unending journey between night and day.

The First Time

Was it really the first time?
How can I be sure?
As the bells begin to chime

With a mountain to climb
How could it endure
Was it really the first time?

It would be a crime
A sickness with no cure,
As the bells begin to chime

No reason or rhyme
The feeling is so pure
Was it really the first time?

Ridiculous or sublime
Can it be secure,
As the bells begin to chime

No words left only mime
Expressing the allure
Was it really the first time?
As the bells begin to chime.

The Sound of Music

The sound of music can make me happy, or sad
Songs remind me of times I cried and times I laughed
Without the sound of music I would have missed so much
By following the music, I saw amazing sights
In places I'd only imagined, so many magical nights
I am grateful for the sound of music
A soundtrack that has accompanied me through life.

The Friend I Never Met

A year like no other has gone by
Everything ground to a halt
Time to reflect and look to the sky
Walking empty streets in solitude
Communication taking place online
A way to stay in touch brings news
Shared photos from a walk or ride
Enjoying a short time outside
A tragic accident brings messages
And new friendships are formed
Helping to move through the grief
Shared interests bring a new belief
Hope of better times ahead
A closeness forms exchanging words
Discovering common ground
Learning to smile, and laugh
Enjoyment can be found
Moving to acceptance but then
The friend I never met is gone
No more words to raise a smile
I am thankful for his friendship

Though it was only for a while
Enriched by everything he shared
Life goes on because he cared.

Bungling Baddies

Joey juddered as the jackhammer jumped
Darren found the drone of the drill dreadful
Terry's telephone trilled through the tunnel
Steven shouted, "Stop stand still."
Willy wondered why we were wavering
Lenny looked longingly at the lock
Sergeant Shaw suddenly shouted, "Stop
Hello, hello, hands high you lot it's a fair cop."

Vistas unfolding

The romance of steam
Passing scenes that were dreams
Now they can be seen

Blue sky up above
Reflected in the river
Hills and trees stand proud

Colours of nature
Fields produce food to nourish
A sight for the soul

Waves pound upon rocks
Mountains sheltering houses
Safety from the storm

It's been a long day
The sun will soon be setting
Time to head for home.

Father's Day

You were my friend and peacekeeper
You taught me how to paint and decorate
How to plant and grow flowers of all kinds
You showed me the meaning of compassion
How you cared about your friends
In times of trouble you rose above it
Always thinking more of others than yourself
When I needed you, you never let me down
I wish you were still here today to sit and talk
I wish we could enjoy just one more long walk.

Freedom

Free to choose or free to lose?
Free to be alone yet not be lonely
Freedom to stand and admire the views
Freedom from thinking about life mostly
We did not choose to come here
We cannot follow our own path
When and where we suddenly appear
Is random with no plan in place, so laugh
Enjoy all the freedom you can find
Whenever you get the opportunity
Sit quietly enjoying the wandering of your mind
But freedom from worry comes from a community
Find friends along the way
To join you for a while
With the freedom to say
I will leave you with a smile.

My First Haiku

Each day, a new pain
Today as well, came the rain
Sun, please come again.

2020

It will get better
That is what I tell myself
Do I believe it?

First it was a shock
Everything I did, ended
Closed signs everywhere

Silence all around
First time out, walking is odd
No people no sound

Early spring colours
Yellow white and purple too
Birds busy building nests

Solitude is nice
I find new activities
Help to pass the time

Six months have gone by
So much time for reflection
Will life be better?

Friends lost others found
Sharing time with me online
I have learnt so much

We should be grateful
Take comfort in the knowledge
Nature will survive.

Whiffling

Whiffling, crawling, sneaking up
Behind the creature he appeared
The creature was not afeard
Whiffling slowly now it came
The creature looked at him
Then whiffled just the same.

Time Flies

Time flies, where does it go?
What's the time?
Time is of the essence.
Time and tide wait for no man
Man in the moon pops up
From time to time
Travelling in time to another time
Watch the time,
Can I watch time?
Time to go; go fast go slow
Turn back the clock
Turn back time
Recall times gone by
Time is a nonsense
Time is relative
Relatives are annoying
Counting the seconds
60 in a minute who decided that?
60 minutes in an hour of 24 to make a day
Time's up
Days, weeks, months, go by
By train or bus or fly?
Time flies.

Too Late to Reconcile

An always uneasy relationship
Broke down four years ago
From time to time it came to mind
Maybe reach out one more time
But no best let it lie
Too much time has passed
What more could be said
Then word came of serious illness
Not expected to recover
He had expressed a wish to see you
As soon as he got home
Send a message to be read to him
When next he is awake
He got to hear those words
There was no response forthcoming
Wife and daughter held his hands
As he slept his final sleep
They had tried to reconnect
And maybe that's enough
There could be no new beginning
It was too late to reconcile.

The Power of Water

The power of water is infinite giving life to all on earth
Its value is incalculable it is precious beyond all worth
It appears in many guises, from tiny droplets to vast oceans
Wherever it is encountered, it stirs up memories and emotions
Splashing through puddles after the rain
Watching droplets slowly descending the window pane
Toes in the sand beneath the gently lapping waves
Eroding the cliffs to form magnificent caves
Landscapes are shaped by the power of rivers
As they descend to the sea from high mountain peaks
Waterfalls, valleys and canyons carved out as it seeks
To return to the oceans and continue this cycle
Aided by powerful allies of gravity, sun and moon
The power of water is infinite giving life to all on earth.

The Life Rooms

The Life Rooms are well named
They give the helpless back their lives
When all is lost and in frustration
They point the way from desperation
It's not an easy journey
With stumbles and mis-steps
But finding strength in those around
Also lost and on the ground
Slowly through the pain and tears
The hopes and dreams appear
Friendships formed, new skills acquired
No longer helpless, now admired
They give us back our lives.

I Disagree

He said it again
"That's just wrong"
"You cannot say that without explaining why it's wrong"
"Yes I can, I'm disagreeing with you because I know it's wrong"
"But you must state your reasoning"
"This is getting us nowhere"
"We should agree to disagree"
"That makes no sense. It's either right or wrong"
"You've never compromised?"
"It's not a compromise if we both believe we are correct and refuse to admit we are wrong"
"Well, what is a compromise?"
"When we each alter our opinion slightly to agree that there is some truth in both statements"
"But I'm right"
"I give up"
"Shall we sit and admire the view?"
"It is rather pleasant."

Lost and Gone Forever

Lost and gone forever
People, places, homes all gone
Into the mists of time

Travels around the globe
Were fun and full of hope
Nothing lasts a lifetime

Pets once loved moved on
Mice, birds and dogs are gone
Lost and gone forever

Homes I loved but moved away
I'll revisit some, I hope one day
Nothing lasts a lifetime

Friendships that didn't last
Fade into the distant past
Lost and gone forever

Interests too that come and go
Football, music, and I used to sew
Nothing lasts a lifetime

A special bond defied the odds
A constant presence that is not
Lost and gone forever
One thing lasts a lifetime.

A Kind of Freedom

Freedom of a certain kind
Is freedom from a busy mind
That very often is inclined
To change course and rewind
Distractions always designed
To stray far and fall behind
Amid unwanted and undefined
Thoughts of nothing but rind
Peeling from fruits maligned
Circling back to those refined
Ideas much more aligned
In order they are enshrined
To bring freedom of a certain kind
The freedom from a busy mind.

Wildlife in the Garden

I took a walk the other day
To somewhere new to me
The early autumn sky clear blue
And sun lighting up the view
Far off beneath a tall tree
A magpie foraged in the grass
A dozing pigeon looked my way
Too comfortable he watched me pass
To my delight I found as I moved on
A wildlife garden island to explore
Moving stealthily along the path
Peeking through the trees
A sight to take my breath away
A large bird sitting tall and proud
As I prepared to take a snap
He heard a noise behind
I thought I'd missed my chance
Continued on to watch bees
Busily collecting nectar
Delicate leaves hanging down
So soft they could have been silk
Then rounding another bend
The fleeing bird appeared again

This time I managed to capture
The beautiful form of a crane
Enjoying the warm tranquility
Basking in the sun by the lake
In the Japanese Garden Island.

Sound and Vision – A Haiku

The song tells it well
The sight and place are eerie
I am moved to tears.

Eternal Migration

Year after year since the beginning of time
Animals have migrated from place to place
Their need to seek out warmer climes
Where with a mate in a safe space?
Another generation will soon arrive

Human beings have also migrated
Since they first set foot upon the earth
Small in number in East Africa located
As numbers grew came a need to set forth
In all directions of the world they strayed

As climates changed in their new lands
So did their appearance change
Living conditions made demands
They adapted with features rearranged
To occupy the world but no-one understands

Humans are one race one species
As it has been proven through DNA
Yet differences in appearance are all they see
Accepting they are only skin deep they may
Finally come to agree it's time to live in peace.

Down to Earth

A breeze loosens the seeds
From the sycamore tree.
Downwards they spiral
Towards the ground
Like uncontrolled helicopters,
Trying to come safely to land
On the ground the sycamore seeds
Are blown along the street.
Dancing as they travel
Amongst passing feet.
They're certainly abundant
And will be quite a feast.
Birds come to inspect.
Are they good enough to eat?

The Fruitless Quest

A pear tree stood proudly
At the end of our garden
When I was a growing child
Every year the pears were picked
Brought into the warm to ripen
They never softened to be eaten
The years went by
The once tall tree
Now broken in two
Had served a purpose
There was nothing more to do
A cloudy day in our scattered country village
The wooden houses keep out the chill
Trees are losing their leaves as autumn arrives.